DEDICATION

to

my father

and

my sister, Joan

OUR FATHER

REVISITED

ROBERT F. MORNEAU

LITURGICAL PRESS   COLLEGEVILLE, MINNESOTA

First printing, 1978
Second printing, 1980

INTRODUCTION

Notes for Prayer

God our Father calls us to prayer that we might be comforted and challenged by his gracious word. This inward journey is not to be taken lightly since it is both a pilgrimage of incomprehensible love and a healing though painful purgation. God speaks his word and we listen; we in turn respond as our Father listens with concern and infinite care. This marvelous mutuality between creator and creature enriches and confirms our spiritual lives. In prayer, God shares his life with us; in prayer, we share our lives with the triune God. Thus the most significant relationship of our lives is deepened by this gentle and candid communication process.

In teaching the disciples how to pray, Jesus directed them to turn to the Father in praise and petition. He taught them the simple and inscrutable prayer we call the *Our Father*. This set of notes provides material for in depth meditation on each section of the Lord's Prayer with the purpose of allowing us to taste more deeply its intrinsic meaning and transparent beauty. These notes can be used in a variety of ways. Were one to make a private retreat, there would be sufficient material here for four hours of prayer for eight days. Were one to use these notes on a daily basis, sufficient references are given for use over a period of a month or more. Others might select various hours of prayer at random, deciding to use this or that section according to what might touch one's immediate experience.

Methodology

In its essence, prayer is a loving attitude and act. Since love has the qualities of spontaneity and freedom, any method of prayer must be cautiously used so as not to block these traits from being part of the prayer experience. Yet, until we have learned the art of prayer, a method can be helpful if it is seen as a means and not an end. The following method will be used in guiding us through the *Our Father:*

a) *Theme.* The theme presents a single, central concern for each hour of prayer. For example, in praying over the petition "Your kingdom come," the theme is "God's kingdom is a kingdom of peace and unity." All of the scriptural references given for this time of prayer support this central thought. The theme is a type of focusing statement and should promote some degree of concentration, attentiveness and simplicity in our prayer.

b) *Desire.* Each theme is followed by a suggested desire. Desires and longings are extremely crucial in our journey to the Father. The novelist Paul Horgan gives sufficient weight to our longings:

A man is more, much more, than bone and blood and meat. Blood and meat we treat alike when we fight a battle, and we give our orders to them, and every man is as useful or not as his neighbor. But when he is hurt or dying or recovering, or longing for whatever it is he longs for, then—then there is something inside him that shows, in ways you cannot put your finger on, and it is the most true thing about him, and the most important.[1]

What we desire from God speaks volumes of who we are and how we interpret life. An example of a desire in terms of the above mentioned theme would be "to see more clearly the Father's kingdom." Thus we approach our Father with enkindled hearts and with holy expectations. Our constant desire is to grow in our knowledge, love and service of our Lord. Though a desire is suggested for every hour of prayer, it would be preferable if individuals would formulate their own desire (longing) in the context of the theme and their own personal lives.

c) *Introduction.* An introductory verse leads into the hour of prayer. Generally, this will be but a single verse or two from scripture which sets the tone for the prayer time. From the start, we should position ourselves in God's presence and ask for the Spirit, the Spirit of faith and worship. The introductory verse allows us to hear God speaking to our hearts and calling us more deeply into his presence. It could well happen that a person would not get beyond this verse for the entire hour of prayer. Fine! What is important is not to pray over all the material given but rather to come before God and simply be with him. Once scripture has served this purpose we set it aside and rest in God in silence and solitude. In every area of life beginnings are important; prayer is no exception. We should begin slowly and reflectively, realizing what we are about and into whose presence we have been drawn. Reverence and awe characterize the prayer experience.

d) *Points.* Having noted the theme and desire, having come before God through the opening verse, we now turn to some extended passages that deal with the topic of prayer. Three selections are given under the heading of "points": two passages from scripture and one from liturgy, the public worship of the Church. The first scriptural reference is taken from either the Old Testament or some book of the New Testament other than the gospel. This selection reflects some aspect of the central theme and invites us to an appropriate response. The second selection is often from the gospel. Here we see how Jesus instructs, bears witness and acts out the Father's love. Of all the "points," this is the most important. The third selection comes from the prayer of the Church. By including this reference, there is a better chance that we will integrate our personal prayer with the public prayer of the entire community. Further, when we celebrate our common liturgy, we will be bringing insights and feelings to that celebration gained through personal reflection in prayer.

e) *Conclusion.* A concluding verse ties up the hour of prayer. This passage touches on the central theme with the hope of pulling together in a short phrase much of what has been pondered and experienced during the hour. At times one might want to memorize the verse as a way of keeping alive the prayer experience during the course of the day. Praise and thanksgiving would be traits which characterize the termination of formal prayer time: praise for who God is in our lives; thanksgiving for what he has done and is doing.

Principles of Prayer

When setting out on a journey, a map and a compass can be handy guides. In venturing into the world of prayer, there are some tools that can be of assistance. These are called principles which give us a sense of direction and help to show the relationships among the various facets of prayer. Five principles are offered for our journey in the *Our Father.*

1. *What we do in prayer is important; what the Spirit does in our hearts is of even greater importance.* One danger for those of us who live in a culture that preaches and practices self-sufficiency is to think that we are the ones who control prayer. Nothing could be further from the truth. Though we must make an effort and exercise discipline in our prayer life, prayer is essentially the

work of God. At bottom, we are the recipients of his over-whelming love. Paradoxically, it is in the "passive" act of receptivity that the deepest form of prayer is experienced. Our principle is confirmed in the writing of St. Paul:

The Spirit too comes to help us in our weakness. For when we cannot choose words in order to pray properly, the Spirit himself expresses our plea in a way that could never be put into words, and God who knows everything in our hearts knows perfectly well what he means, and that the pleas of the saints expressed by the Spirit are according to the mind of God (Rom. 8:26-27).

2. *In prayer, we must be aware of who we are, to whom we speak, and the topic of dialogue.* Though this principle may seem simple and obvious upon first reading, it is most difficult to put into practice. The assumptions of the principle are that we have a fairly well developed degree of self-knowledge, that we know basically who the living and true God is, and that there is some clarity about the mystery of the dialogue. These assumptions must be carefully looked into. A reverse principle can also be stated within this context: a major cause for sterility in prayer results from our coming to prayer with a false self or to approach a god in prayer who does not exist. How different is our real self from our ideal or social self; how different is the Father that Jesus reveals to us from the god presented in the thoughts of the Pharisees. No communication is possible when one of the two parties is non-existent. Further, the topic of conversation must be realistic and relevant to one's life. Teresa of Avila provides the source for this principle:

As far as I can understand, the door of entry into this castle is prayer and meditation: I do not say mental prayer rather than vocal, for, if it is prayer at all, it must be accompanied by meditation. If a person does not think Whom he is addressing, and what he is asking for, and who it is that is asking and of Whom he is asking it, I do not consider that he is praying at all even though he be constantly moving his lips.[2]

3. *Quality is the norm, not quantity.* Another way of expressing this principle is to say "feed on little." If someone were to say that during one hour of prayer six chapters of St. John's Gospel were covered, we would rightly question the validity and quality of the prayer. If a person would cover six verses of chapter one of John's Gospel and do so with reflective attentiveness, there is high probability that the prayer was meaningful and of good quality. It is important, therefore, that in the notes that follow

the tendency to cover it all be avoided. Purposely, more material is given than what is necessary so that people might have the option of choosing passages that are most pertinent to their life. In support of this principle, we turn to a passage from St. Ignatius' *Spiritual Exercises:*

> For it is not much knowledge that fills and satisfies the soul, but the intimate understanding and relish of the Truth.[3]

4. *Nail things down!* Much of prayer can be nebulous and ambiguous unless some form of specificity is present. Some will find it helpful and important to write down passages that touch their heart; others will have a need to express to a director the feelings and thoughts that arise in prayer. Explication is important, for unless things are written down, spoken to another, or acted out, they tend to be only half real. Prayer is no exception. Keeping a prayer journal can be advantageous in our growth in prayer. Entries can be made either during prayer time itself or, upon conclusion, a summary statement can be entered, capturing as best as possible the experience of the Lord. Simone Weil wrote that "no thought attains to its fullest existence unless it is incarnated in a human environment"; by nailing things down in word or deed we continue to grow in clarity and simplicity.

5. *Avoid repression as much as possible; be honest.* Teresa's reverential boldness is an apt model:

> "How is it, my God," I have said to Him, "that it is not enough for Thee to keep me in this miserable life, which I endure for love of Thee, willing to live where on every hand there are obstacles to my having fruition of Thee? I have to eat, sleep, attend to my business and mix with people of every kind—and all this is the sorest torment to me. How few are the moments which remain to me for enjoying communion with Thee, and even during those moments Thou hidest Thyself! How does this agree with Thy mercy? How can Thy love for me endure it? Verily, Lord, I believe that, if it were possible for me to hide myself from Thee as Thou hidest Thyself from me, the Love that Thou bearest me is such that Thou wouldst not endure it. But Thou art with me and seest me always. My Lord, this is not to be borne; consider, I beseech Thee, what a wrong is being done to one who so much loves Thee."[4]

Teresa's prayer was honest and candid; no repression but simple recording of what passed through her heart. We must be careful that we do not deny certain "unacceptable" movements and thoughts that occur in prayer out of apparent respect for God. God wants us to be honest and to talk everything over as it is. Repression destroys prayer's authenticity. Raïssa Maritain writes in her journal: "I enter into the presence of God with all my load of misery and troubles. And he takes me just as I am and makes me to be alone with Him."[5] Gideon gives us another example of honest prayer:

> ...when the angel of Yahweh appeared to him and said, 'Yahweh is with you, valiant warrior!' Gideon answered him, 'Forgive me, my lord, but if Yahweh is with us, then why is it that all this is happening to us now? And where are all the wonders our ancestors tell us of when they say, "Did not Yahweh bring us out of Egypt?" But now Yahweh has deserted us; he has abandoned us to Midian' (Jg. 6:12-13).

Avoidance of repression means that we bring our true self to prayer; only then can the Lord's healing and loving touch transform us.

[1]Paul Horgan, *A Distant Trumpet* (New York: Farrar, Straus and Cudahy, 1951), p. 225.

[2]*The Complete Works of St. Teresa.* Translated and edited by E. Allison Peers. Volume II (London: Sheed and Ward, 1944), pp. 203-204.

[3]Louis J. Puhl, S.J., *The Spiritual Exercises of St. Ignatius* (Chicago: Loyola U. Press, 1951) , p. 2.

[4]*The Complete Works of St. Teresa, op. cit.,* Volume I, p. 265.

[5]*Raïssa's Journal.* Presented by Jacques Maritain (Albany, N.Y.: Magi Books, Inc., 1963), p. 225.

Day of Faith in God Our Father

"Our Father in heaven,
may your name be held holy"
(Mt. 6 : 9)

ABBA

FATHER

First Hour —
   Theme: What is our Father like?
   Desire: To know the Father of our Lord Jesus Christ!

INTRODUCTION
   Pause and realize that God will speak now through scripture. Ask for the Spirit of faith and worship at the beginning of prayer. Let God take the initiative: he speaks first, we listen and then respond. The prophet assures us that we are never abandoned or forgotten — what a mystery!

   For Zion was saying, 'Yahweh has abandoned me,
   the Lord has forgotten me'.
   Does a woman forget her baby at the breast,
   or fail to cherish the son of her womb?
   Yet even if these forget,
   I will never forget you.

1

See, I have branded you on the palms of my hands,
Your ramparts are always under my eye.

(Is. 49:14-19)

POINTS

• We come to know the Father through Jesus. Allow Jesus to
reveal what his Father is like — what *our* Father is like. Focus on
the Father's mind and heart as he longs for the return of his
child ... the love, the concern, the forgiveness, the joy.

He also said, 'A man had two sons. The younger
said to his father, "Father, let me have the share of
the estate that would come to me." So the father
divided the property between them. A few days
later, the younger son got together everything he
had and left for a distant country where he
squandered his money on a life of debauchery.
'When he had spent it all, that country experienced
a severe famine, and now he began to feel the
pinch, so he hired himself out to one of the local
inhabitants who put him on his farm to feed the
pigs. And he would willingly have filled his belly
with the husks the pigs were eating but no one
offered him anything. Then he came to his senses
and said, "How many of my father's paid servants
have more food than they want, and here am I
dying of hunger! I will leave this place and go to
my father and say: Father, I have sinned against
heaven and against you; I no longer deserve to be
called your son; treat me as one of your paid
servants." So he left the place and went back to his
father.
'While he was still a long way off, his father saw
him and was moved with pity. He ran to the boy,
clasped him in his arms and kissed him tenderly.
Then his son said, "Father, I have sinned against
heaven and against you. I no longer deserve to be
called your son." But the father said to his
servants, "Quick! Bring out the best robe and put it
on him; put a ring on his finger and sandals on his
feet. Bring the calf we have been fattening, and kill
it; we are going to have a feast, a celebration,

2

because this son of mine was dead and has come
back to life; he was lost and is found." And they
began to celebrate.'

(Lk. 15:11-24)

• How often Jesus prayed this psalm! Allow him to lead you
now as he describes how the Father guided, nourished and
cared for him on his journey. Indeed, we lack nothing if we
surrender our lives to the good Shepherd.

Yahweh is my shepherd,
I lack nothing.
In meadows of green grass he lets me lie.
To the waters of repose he leads me;
there he revives my soul.
He guides me by paths of virtue
for the sake of his name.
Though I pass through a gloomy valley,
I fear no harm;
beside me your rod and your staff
are there, to hearten me.
You prepare a table before me
under the eyes of my enemies;
you anoint my head with oil,
my cup brims over.
Ah, how goodness and kindness pursue me,
every day of my life;
my home, the house of Yahweh,
as long as I live!

(Ps. 23)

LITURGY
The Church honors the Father in the *Gloria.* Let these words
flow from the heart as we join in this eternal hymn of praise:

Glory to God in the highest,
and peace to his people on earth.
Lord God, heavenly King, Almighty God and Father,
we worship you, we give you thanks,
we praise you for your glory.

CONCLUSION
Our call is to be like the Father!

He, Yahweh, is merciful, tenderhearted,

3

slow to anger, very loving,
and universally kind; Yahweh's tenderness
embraces all his creatures.

(Ps. 145: 8-9)

Second Hour —
  Theme: The Father is OUR common Father.
  Desire: To grow in our solidarity as his children-people.

INTRODUCTION
  We enter God's presence with reverence and awe. He will speak. At the start of prayer we are called to unite ourselves with Jesus in coming to the Father. Ask for the power of the Spirit to enlighten our minds, enkindle our hearts.

Know that he, Yahweh, is God,
he made us and we belong to him,
we are his people, the flock that he pastures.

(Ps. 100:3)

POINTS
  • Join Mary. Ponder the great message given her — my Father, your Father. The Father of all creation and history.

Meanwhile Mary stayed outside near the tomb, weeping. Then still weeping, she stooped to look inside, and saw two angels in white sitting where the body of Jesus had been, one at the head, the other at the feet. They said, 'Woman, why are you weeping?' 'They have taken my Lord away' she replied 'and I don't know where they have put him.' As she said this she turned around and saw Jesus standing there, though she did not recognize him. Jesus said, 'Woman, why are you weeping? Who are you looking for?' Supposing him to be the gardener, she said, 'Sir, if you have taken him away, tell me where you have put him, and I will go and remove him'. Jesus said, 'Mary!' She knew him then and said to him in Hebrew, "Rabbuni!" — which means Master. Jesus said to her, 'Do not cling to me, because I have not yet ascended to the Father. But go and find the brothers, and tell them: I am ascending to my Father and your Father, to

4

my God and your God.' So Mary of Magdala went
and told the disciples that she had seen the Lord
and that he had said these things to her.

(Jn. 20:11-18)

• We are empowered to say "Abba." We are given a common
Spirit. We are members of the same family and heirs,with Jesus.

Everyone moved by the Spirit is a son of God. The
spirit you received is not the spirit of slaves
bringing fear into your lives again; it is the spirit of
sons, and it makes us cry out, 'Abba, Father!' The
Spirit himself and our spirit bear united witness
that we are children of God. And if we are children
we are heirs as well: heirs of God and coheirs with
Christ, sharing his sufferings so as to share his
glory.

(Rom. 8:14-17)

LITURGY

Penitential Rite: with all the Church we come to our Father. "I
confess to almighty God, and to you, *my brothers and sisters.*"

CONCLUSION

Look down from heaven, look down from your
holy and glorious dwelling. Where is your ardour,
your might, the yearning of your inmost heart? Do
not let your compassion go unmoved, for you are
our Father.

(Is. 63:15)

———————————

Third Hour —

Theme: Our Father is with us and for us.
Desire: To experience his intimacy and presence.

INTRODUCTION

What a great mystery! We must never take for granted God's
closeness to us. He is with us *here* and *now.* Surrender to his
presence, letting all fear go.

Do not be afraid, for I have redeemed you;
I have called you by your name, you are mine.

(Is. 43:1)

5

• Note God's constant call and fidelity. His kindness and deep love are ever near. Why is there so much blindness and deafness?

When Israel was a child I loved him,
and I called my son out of Egypt.
But the more I called to them,
    the further they went from me;
they have offered sacrifices to the Baals
and set their offerings smoking before the idols.
I myself taught Ephraim to walk,
I took them in my arms;
yet they have not understood
    that I was the one looking after them.
I led them with reins of kindness,
with leading-strings of love.
I was like someone who lifts an infant
    close against his cheek;
stooping down to him I gave him his food.
They will have to go back to Egypt,
Assyria must be their king,
because they have refused to return to me.
The sword will rage through their towns,
wiping out their children,
glutting itself inside their fortresses.

(Hos. 11:1-6)

• Jesus reveals the plan of the Father. The Father dwells among us and the Trinity makes their home within us. When they come, what happens? What is happening now? Do I really believe in this promise of presence? What is the level of my hospitality, openness, surrender?

Jesus replied: 'If anyone loves me he will keep my word, and my Father will love him, and we shall come to him and make our home with him.'

(Jn. 14:23)

LITURGY

Taste deeply the rich theology in this prayer said by the priest before communion:

Lord Jesus Christ, Son of the living God, by the will of the Father and the work of the Holy Spirit your death brought life to the world. By your holy

6

body and blood free me from all my sins and from every evil. Keep me faithful to your teaching, and never let me be parted from you.

CONCLUSION

With the psalmist we respond to what the Father has and is doing for us here and now. We are to celebrate and rejoice in his love.

I will celebrate your love for ever, Yahweh,
age after age my words
    shall proclaim your faithfulness;
for I claim that love is built to last for ever
and your faithfulness founded firmly in the heavens.

(Ps. 89:1-2)

Fourth Hour —

Theme: The Father's name is holy (name = person).
Desire: To revere the person of the Father always.

INTRODUCTION

Prayer demands taking time, pausing, being quiet. Beg for the gift of interior silence and loving attention (contemplation). Only in silence can we hear. Come to know God now, for he speaks.

Pause a while and know that I am God,
exalted among the nations, exalted over the earth!

(Ps. 46:10)

POINTS

• What deep respect Jesus has for the name of his Father. His name, his person is the center of Jesus' life; an abiding consciousness of who the Father is. What/who is my center?

'Now, Father, it is time for you to glorify me
with that glory I had with you
before the world ever was.
I have made your name known
to the men you took from the world to give me.
They were yours and you gave them to me,
and they have kept your word.
I am not in the world any longer,
but they are in the world,
and I am coming to you.

Holy Father,
keep those you have given me true to your name,
so that they may be one like us.
While I was with them,
I kept those you had given me true to your name.
I have watched over them and not one is lost
except the one who chose to be lost,
and this was to fulfill the scriptures.
Father, Righteous One,
the world has not known you,
but I have known you,
and these have known
that you have sent me.
I have made your name known to them
and will continue to make it known,
so that the love with which you loved me
    may be in them,
and so that I may be in them.'

(Jn. 17:5-6, 11-12, 25-26)

• Join Moses as he encounters God. Prayer is going up the mountain; here the Father reveals his name to us. We must truly desire and long for this knowledge and love. What deep reverence Moses had!

Then Moses said to God, 'I am to go, then, to the sons of Israel and say to them,"The God of your fathers has sent me to you". But if they ask me what his name is, what am I to tell them?' And God said to Moses, 'I Am who I Am. This' he added 'is what you must say to the sons of Israel: "I Am has sent me to you".' And God also said to Moses, 'You are to say to the sons of Israel: "Yahweh, the God of your fathers, the God of Abraham, the God of Isaac, and the God of Jacob, has sent me to you". This is my name for all time; by this name I shall be invoked for all generations to come.

(Ex. 3:13-15)

LITURGY

Dwell silently on the sign of the cross with which we start our liturgy. Unpack the depth of this gesture and sign:

8

In the name of the Father, and of the Son,
and of the Holy Spirit.

CONCLUSION

How great is your name! Be proud of God.

Yahweh, our Lord.
how great your name throughout the earth!

(Ps. 8:1)

———————————

Day of Hope in the Coming of God's Kingdom

"Your kingdom come" (Mt. 6:10)

First Hour —
> Theme: God's kingdom is a kingdom of peace and unity.
> Desire: To see more clearly the Father's kingdom.

INTRODUCTION

Ask for the spirit of prayer. God speaks to us through the scriptures in a special way. We must listen intently and lovingly. Who is this child? What will he do?

> For there is a child born for us,
> a son given to us
> and dominion is laid on his shoulders;
> and this is the name they gave him:
> Wonder-Counsellor, Mighty-God,
> Eternal-Father, Prince-of-Peace.
>
> (Is. 9:5-6)

POINTS

• The Old Testament foreshadows the New Testament. Solomon foreshadows Jesus. Peace and quiet will come. The task: to build a house for Yahweh. This is our task now.

> "But now a son is born to you. He shall be a man of peace, and I will give him peace from all the

enemies that surround him; for Solomon is his
name, and in his days I will give Israel peace and
quiet. He shall build a house for my name; he shall
be a son to me and I a father to him, and I will
make his royal throne secure in Israel for ever."
Now, my son, may Yahweh be with you and give
you success in building a house for Yahweh your
God, as he has said concerning you. Yet may he
give you discretion and discernment, may he give
you his orders for Israel so that you may observe
the Law of Yahweh your God. Success will be
yours if you carefully observe the statutes and the
ordinances that Yahweh has prescribed to Moses
for Israel. Be strong and stand fast, be fearless, be
dauntless.

(1 Chr. 22:9-13)

• Travel up the mountain with the crowds. Sit quietly as Jesus
reveals to us NOW what the kingdom is like. There is no true
happiness outside the Kingdom. Listen carefully as Jesus speaks
to you. Respond in praise and love.

Seeing the crowds, he went up the hill. There he sat
down and was joined by his disciples. Then he began to
speak. This is what he taught them:
'How happy are the poor in spirit;
theirs is the kingdom of heaven.
Happy the gentle:
they shall have the earth for their heritage.
Happy those who mourn:
they shall be comforted.
Happy those who hunger and thirst for what is right:
they shall be satisfied.
Happy the merciful:
they shall have mercy shown them.
Happy the pure in heart:
they shall see God.
Happy the peacemakers:
they shall be called sons of God.
Happy those who are persecuted in the cause of right:
theirs is the kingdom of heaven.'

(Mt. 5:1-10)

With the Church we pray:

Then, in your kingdom, freed from the corruption
of sin and death, we shall sing your glory with
every creature through Christ our Lord.

(Canon IV)

CONCLUSION
God's peace is universal and eternal. Pray this psalm with
Jesus.

In his days virtue will flourish,
   a universal peace till the moon is no more;
his empire shall stretch from sea to sea,
   from the river to the ends of the earth.

(Ps. 72:7-8)

Second Hour —
   Theme: Christ is our King.
   Desire: To serve our Lord more completely.

INTRODUCTION
Enter into prayer with reverence. God speaks his word here
and now. Pray for the gift of silence. Like Jesus, these words
apply to our lives.

Let me proclaim Yahweh's decree;
he has told me, 'You are my son,
today I have become your father.
Ask and I will give you the nations for your heritage,
the ends of the earth for your domain.'

(Ps. 2:7-8)

POINTS
   • Christ the king is no medieval monarch. He is a humble,
serving shepherd. Do not take this for granted. He lays down
his life for me. Is this really true? Ponder the mystery.

I am the good shepherd:
the good shepherd is one
who lays down his life for his sheep.
The hired man, since he is not the shepherd
and the sheep do not belong to him,
abandons the sheep and runs away
as soon as he sees a wolf coming,

and then the wolf attacks and scatters the sheep;
this is because he is only a hired man
and has no concern for the sheep.
I am the good shepherd;
I know my own
and my own know me,
just as the Father knows me
and I know the Father;
and I lay down my life for my sheep.

(Jn. 10:11-15)

• Peter boldly explains the mystery of our faith. Sit in the audience and listen. What do these words mean to you? Jesus is Lord! Does he reign in my life?

Brothers, no one can deny that the patriarch David himself is dead and buried: his tomb is still with us. But since he was a prophet, and knew that God had sworn him an oath to make one of his descendants succeed him on the throne, what he foresaw and spoke about was the resurrection of Christ: he is the one who was not abandoned to Hades, and whose body did not experience corruption. God raised this man Jesus to life, and all of us are witnesses to that. Now raised to the heights by God's right hand, he has received from the Father the Holy Spirit, who was promised, and what you see and hear is the outpouring of that Spirit. For David himself never went up to heaven; and yet these works are his:
The Lord said to my Lord;
Sit at my right hand
until I make your enemies
a footstool for you.
'For this reason the whole House of Israel can be certain that God has made this Jesus whom you crucified both Lord and Christ.'

(Acts 2:29-36)

LITURGY
The prayer before communion speaks profoundly of the kingdom:

Lord Jesus Christ, you said to your apostles: I leave

13

you peace, my peace I give you. Look not on our sins, but on the faith of your Church, and grant us the peace and unity of your kingdom where you live for ever and ever.

CONCLUSION

Ponder this vision of the prophet. Praise God for his goodness and fidelity.

He will stand and feed his flock
with the power of Yahweh, with the majesty of
the name of his God.
They will live secure, for from then on
he will extend his power
to the ends of the land.
He himself will be peace.

(Mic. 5:4-5)

Third Hour —
Theme: Servants of the kingdom.
Desire: To appreciate those who built up the kingdom.

INTRODUCTION

Prayer is listening to God's word and responding from the heart. Realize that God speaks now through scripture. Ponder his presence and respond in praise and thanksgiving.

After that will come the end, when he hands over the kingdom to God the Father, having done away with every sovereignty, authority and power. For he must be king until he has put all his enemies under his feet and the last of the enemies to be destroyed is death, for everything is to be put under his feet. Though when it is said that everything is subjected, this clearly cannot include the One who subjected everything to him. And when everything is subjected to him, then the Son himself will be subject in his turn to the One who subjected all things to him, so that God may be all in all.

(1 Cor. 15:24-28)

• God loved and called David. What a responsibility! David, God's servant, was not "perfect." God continues to call today. *You* are the person to shepherd my people. What a mystery, grace, privilege, responsibility!

> All the tribes of Israel then came to David at Hebron. 'Look' they said 'we are your own flesh and blood. In days past when Saul was our king, it was you who led Israel in all their exploits; and Yahweh said to you, "You are the man who shall be shepherd of my people Israel, you shall be the leader of Israel".' So all the elders of Israel came to the king at Hebron, and King David made a pact with them at Hebron in the presence of Yahweh, and they anointed David king of Israel.
>
> David was thirty years old when he became king, and he reigned for forty years. He reigned in Hebron over Judah for seven years and six months; then he reigned in Jerusalem over all Israel and Judah for thirty-three years.

(2 Sam. 5:1-5)

• Listen in on this beautiful dialogue between Jesus and Peter. Note the pain and then the call to obedience. Does the risen Lord really lead in my life? Am I truly a servant? Would Peter have chosen what the Lord asked? Don't be afraid to question in prayer.

> After the meal Jesus said to Simon Peter, 'Simon son of John, do you love me more than these others do?' He answered, 'Yes Lord, you know that I love you'. Jesus said to him, 'Feed my lambs'. A second time he said to him, 'Simon son of John, do you love me?' He replied, 'Yes Lord, you know I love you'. Jesus said to him, 'Look after my sheep'. Then he said to him a third time, 'Simon son of John, do you love me?' Peter was upset that he asked him the third time, 'Do you love me?' and said, 'Lord, you know everything; you know I love you'. Jesus said to him, 'Feed my sheep.
>
> I tell you most solemnly,
> when you were young

you put on your own belt
and walked where you liked;
but when you grow old
you will stretch out your hands,
and somebody else will put a belt around you
and take you where you would rather not go.'
In these words he indicated the kind of death by
which Peter would give glory to God. After this he
said, 'Follow me'.

Peter turned and saw the disciple Jesus loved
following them—the one who had leaned on his
breast at the supper and had said to him, 'Lord,
who is it that will betray you?' Seeing him, Peter
said to Jesus, 'What about him, Lord?' Jesus
answered, 'If I want him to stay behind till I come,
what does it matter to you? You are to follow me.'
The rumour then went out among the brothers
that this disciple would not die. Yet Jesus had not
said to Peter, 'He will not die', but, 'If I want him to
stay behind till I come'.

(Jn. 21:15-23)

LITURGY
On the feast of Christ the King we pray:

Almighty and merciful God, you break the power
of evil and make all things new in your Son Jesus
Christ, the King of the universe. May all in heaven
and earth acclaim your glory and never cease to
praise you.

CONCLUSION
Paul was a true servant of Christ. He knew that the kingdom
of God was one of power, not just words. Ask God to
strengthen you as he did Paul.

When it seemed that I was not coming to visit you,
some of you became self-important, but I will be
visiting you soon, the Lord willing, and then I shall
want to know not what these self-important people
have to say, but what they can do, since the
kingdom of God is not just words, it is power. It is

for you to decide: do I come with a stick in my
hand or in a spirit of love and goodwill?

(1 Cor. 4:18-21)

Fourth Hour —
Theme: The NOWNESS of the kingdom.
Desire: To experience the closeness of God's reign and to
surrender to his call.

INTRODUCTION

Prayer is a time of loving attention to God. Through scripture
we are drawn into his presence. Once there, drop everything,
even scripture. In silence rest in the Father's embrace. The
kingdom is now; be with the Father.

'See, the days are coming—it is Yahweh who speaks—
when I will raise a virtuous Branch for David,
who will reign as true king and be wise,
practising honesty and integrity in the land.
In his days Judah will be saved
and Israel dwell in confidence.
And this is the name he will be called:
Yahweh-our-integrity.'

(Jer. 23:5-6)

POINTS

• Jesus is teacher. What is the kingdom like? So simple, so
profound. Ask the Father to reveal the inner meaning of these
parables. Don't figure them out.

He put another parable before them. 'The kingdom of
heaven is like a mustard seed which a man took and
sowed in his field. It is the smallest of all seeds, but
when it has grown it is the biggest shrub of all and
becomes a tree so that the birds of the air come and
shelter in its branches.'
He told them another parable. 'The kingdom of
heaven is like the yeast a woman took and mixed in
with three measures of flour till it was leavened all
through'.

(Mt. 13:31-33)

• The kingdom of God is very near. It is already upon us. The

17

kingdom is as near as our neighbor. Ponder these words. Trust that God will fulfill them in your life.

Then the King will say to those on his right hand, "Come, you whom my Father has blessed, take for your heritage the kingdom prepared for you since the foundation of the world. For I was hungry and you gave me food; I was thirsty and you gave me drink; I was a stranger and you made me welcome; naked and you clothed me, sick and you visited me, in prison and you came to see me."

(Mt. 25:34-36)

LITURGY

Listen to Origen's prayer on the feast of Christ the King:

It is clear that he who prays for the coming of God's kingdom prays rightly to have it within himself, that there it might grow and bear fruit and become perfect. For God reigns in each of his holy ones. Anyone is holy who obeys the spiritual laws of God, who dwells in him as in a well-ordered city. The Father is present in the perfect soul, and with him Christ reigns, according to the words: We shall come to him and make our home with him.

CONCLUSION

A kingdom of faithfulness and integrity that is present NOW. Praise God.

Yahweh Sabaoth says this. Now I am going to save my people from the countries of the East and from the countries of the West. I will bring them back to live inside Jerusalem. They shall be my people and I will be their God in faithfulness and integrity.

(Zech. 8:7-8)

Day of Surrender to God's Will

"Your will be done" (Mt. 6:10)

First Hour —
    Theme: Jesus does the Father's will.
    Desire: To participate more fully in the paschal mystery.

INTRODUCTION

Prayer is God seeking us, we seeking God. In faith, he draws near. Listen as the Father reveals to us what his son is like.

God, you are my God, I am seeking you,
my soul is thirsting for you,
my flesh is longing for you,
a land parched, weary and waterless;
I long to gaze on you in the Sanctuary,
and to see your power and glory.

(Ps. 63:1-2)

POINTS

• With reverence and awe be present with the Lord in his agony. Jesus did not look forward to suffering, yet he accepted it for our salvation. He would pay the price. Respond in deep, humble gratitude.

He then left to make his way as usual to the Mount of Olives, with the disciples following. When they

19

reached the place he said to them, 'Pray not to be put to the test'.

Then he withdrew from them, about a stone's throw away, and knelt down and prayed. 'Father,' he said 'if you are willing, take this cup away from me. Nevertheless, let your will be done, not mine.' Then an angel appeared to him, coming from heaven to give him strength. In his anguish he prayed even more earnestly, and his sweat fell to the ground like great drops of blood.

When he rose from prayer he went to the disciples and found them sleeping for sheer grief. 'Why are you asleep?' he said to them. 'Get up and pray not to be put to the test.'

(Lk. 22:39-46)

• What a revelation! Here is God's plan and will — eternal life. This is why Jesus was sent. Pray for the gift of understanding the depth of this mystery.

All that the Father gives me will come to me,
and whoever comes to me
I shall not turn him away;
because I have come from heaven,
not to do my own will,
but to do the will of the one who sent me.
Now the will of him who sent me
is that I should lose nothing
of all that he has given to me,
and that I should raise it up on the last day.
Yes, it is my Father's will
that whoever sees the Son and believes in him
shall have eternal life,
and that I shall raise him up on the last day.

(Jn. 6:37-40)

LITURGY

The Eucharist draws our attention to the Father's will:

In fulfillment of your will he gave himself up to death; but by rising from the dead, he destroyed death and restored life.

(Canon IV)

CONCLUSION

What happened in the life of Jesus also happened in the life of St. Paul. Pray also to participate in the living out of the paschal mystery: the life, death and resurrection of Jesus. By doing this we glorify our Father.

> When we heard this, we and everybody there implored Paul not to go to Jerusalem. To this he replied, 'What are you trying to do—weaken my resolution by your tears? For my part, I am ready not only to be tied up but even to die in Jerusalem for the name of the Lord Jesus.' And so, as he would not be persuaded, we gave up the attempt, saying, 'The Lord's will be done'.

(Acts 21:12-14)

Second Hour —

Theme: Mary does the Father's will.
Desire: To share in Mary's openness and generosity.

INTRODUCTION

Join Mary in praising Yahweh. His light guides our prayer. In prayer we have nothing to fear; God is our strength.

> Yahweh is my light and my salvation,
>   whom need I fear?
> Yahweh is the fortress of my life,
>   of whom should I be afraid?
> When evil men advance against me
>   to devour my flesh,
> they, my opponents, my enemies,
>   are the ones who stumble and fall.

(Ps. 27:1-2)

POINTS

• Go slowly. Pray this passage as if for the first time. Incredible! God's great love entering so profoundly into history. Mary's generosity in doing whatever the Father asks.

> 'The Holy Spirit will come upon you' the angel answered 'and the power of the Most High will cover you with its shadow. And so the child will be holy and will be called Son of God. Know this too:

21

your kinswoman Elizabeth has, in her old age, herself conceived a son, and she whom people called barren is now in her sixth month, for nothing is impossible to God.' 'I am the handmaid of the Lord,' said Mary 'let what you have said be done to me.' And the angel left her.

(Lk. 1:35-38)

• Mary does the Father's will completely. The cross and pain are embraced. What a price she is willing to pay; what deep love she has received and returns. Join Mary at the cross — in silence.

Near the cross of Jesus stood his mother and his mother's sister, Mary the wife of Clopas, and Mary of Magdala. Seeing his mother and the disciple he loved standing near her, Jesus said to his mother, 'Woman, this is your son'. Then to the disciple he said, 'This is your mother'. And from that moment the disciple made a place for her in his home.

(Jn. 19:25-27)

LITURGY
In faith we profess:

For us men and for our salvation he came down from heaven; by the power of the Holy Spirit he was born of the Virgin Mary and became man.

(Creed)

CONCLUSION
Note the depth of God's will. Our finite minds falter before the mystery. Only in faith can we hope to fulfill what the Father asks of us. Praise and worship our God, the God of truth and goodness.

How rich are the depths of God—how deep his wisdom and knowledge—and how impossible to penetrate his motives or understand his methods! Who could ever know the mind of the Lord? Who could ever be his counsellor? Who could ever give him anything? All that exists comes from him; all is by him and for him. To him be glory for ever! Amen.

(Rom. 11:33-36)

Third Hour —

Theme: Opposition to God's will.

Desire: To realize the forces within ourselves and in the world that oppose God's loving plan.

INTRODUCTION

In prayer I must bring the real, personal me (not some imagined self) to the Father of our Lord Jesus Christ. Scripture reveals the mind and heart of God. We must listen and respond with reverence. To live in the darkness of lies and untruth is to be a fool.

The fool says in his heart,
'There is no God!'
They are false, corrupt, vile,
there is not one good man left.
God is looking down from heaven
at the sons of men,
to see if a single one is wise,
if a single one is seeking God.

(Ps. 53:1-2)

POINTS

• God's plan for a great harvest. What went wrong? Why the sour grapes? Review what God has done for you. What have been the results?

Let me sing to my friend
the song of his love for his vineyard.
My friend had a vineyard
on a fertile hillside.
He dug the soil, cleared it of stones,
and planted choice vines in it.
In the middle he built a tower,
he dug a press here too.
He expected it to yield grapes,
but sour grapes were all that it gave.
And now, inhabitants of Jerusalem
and men of Judah,
I ask you to judge
between my vineyard and me.
What could I have done for my vineyard
that I have not done?

23

I expected it to yield grapes.
Why did it yield sour grapes instead?

(Is. 5:1-4)

• God's will is evidenced in a certain climate or spirit. So too is the enemy's. History verifies what Paul writes about as do our own times, our own lives.

Let me put it like this: if you are guided by the Spirit you will be in no danger of yielding to self-indulgence, since self-indulgence is the opposite of the Spirit, the Spirit is totally against such a thing, and it is precisely because the two are so opposed that you do not always carry out your good intentions. If you are led by the Spirit, no law can touch you. When self-indulgence is at work the results are obvious: fornication, gross indecency and sexual irresponsibility; idolatry and sorcery; feuds and wrangling, jealousy, bad temper and quarrels; disagreements, factions, envy; drunkenness, orgies and similar things. I warn you now, as I warned you before: those who behave like this will not inherit the kingdom of God.

(Gal. 5:16-21)

LITURGY

With the Christian community we recognize that God's will has not been fully lived and so we pray:

"Lord, we have sinned against you.
    Lord, have mercy.
Lord, show us your mercy and love.
    And grant us your salvation."

CONCLUSION

We must stand firm against whatever opposes the will of the Father. The Lord gives us strength and hope.

Happy the man who stands firm when trials come. He has proved himself, and will win the prize of life, the crown that the Lord has promised to those who love him.

(Jas. 1:12)

Fourth Hour —
Theme: Our response to God's will.
Desire: To honestly evaluate our life in Christ.

INTRODUCTION
   Christian prayer is characterized by joy and gladness. Prayer means to be with God and no greater joy can be had. Indeed, "God is great" and he longs to communicate his love and forgiveness to us.

But joy and gladness
   for all who seek you!
To all who love your saving power
   give constant cause to say, 'God is great!'

(Ps. 40:16)

POINTS
   • Paul describes God's plan of salvation. We are challenged to "live through love in his presence," to foster unity and peace, to reconcile the world to the Father, to love deeply, to do the Father's will in our lives.

Blessed be God the Father of our Lord Jesus Christ,
   who has blessed us with all the spiritual blessings
      of heaven in Christ,
Before the world was made, he chose us,
   chose us in Christ,
to be holy and spotless, and to live through love
   in his presence,
determining that we should become his adopted sons,
   through Jesus Christ
for his own kind purposes,
to make us praise the glory of his grace,
his free gift to us in the Beloved,
in whom, through his blood, we gain our freedom,
   the forgiveness of our sins.
Such is the richness of the grace
which he has showered on us
in all wisdom and insight.
He has let us know the mystery of his purpose,
the hidden plan he so kindly made in Christ
   from the beginning

to act upon when the times had run their course
    to the end;
everything in the heavens and everything on earth.
And it is in him that we were claimed as God's own,
chosen from the beginning,
under the predetermined plan of the one
    who guides all things
as he decides by his own will;
chosen to be,
for his greater glory,
the people who would put their hopes in Christ
    before he came.
Now you too, in him,
have heard the message of the truth
    and the good news of your salvation,
and have believed it;
and you too have been stamped with the seal
    of the Holy Spirit of the Promise,
the pledge of our inheritance
which brings freedom for those whom God
    has taken for his own,
to make his glory praised.

(Eph. 1:3-14)

• Are we living out God's will? Paul gives us nine signs to discern this question. Only through the gift of the Spirit can we continue to grow in these virtues. "Lord, send forth your Spirit. Come, Lord Jesus!"

> What the Spirit brings is very different: love, joy, peace, patience, kindness, goodness, trustfulness, gentleness and self-control. There can be no law against things like that, of course. You cannot belong to Christ Jesus unless you crucify all self-indulgent passions and desires.
>
> Since the Spirit is our life, let us be directed by the Spirit. We must stop being conceited, provocative and envious.

(Gal. 5:22-26)

LITURGY

    The liturgy reveals the source of our power in doing the Father's will:

And that we might live no longer for ourselves but
for him, he sent the Holy Spirit from you, Father,
as his first gift to those who believe, to complete
his work on earth and bring us the fullness of
grace.

(Canon IV)

CONCLUSION

God's will for us is to love. He first loved us and we receive
that precious gift to pass on to others.

We ourselves have known and put our faith in
God's love towards ourselves.
God is love
and anyone who lives in love lives in God,
and God lives in him.

(1 Jn. 4:16)

Day of Rejoicing in God's Daily Bread

"Give us today our daily bread"

(Mt. 6:11)

First Hour —
  Theme: The bread of the Eucharist.
  Desire: To taste and see the goodness of the Lord.

INTRODUCTION

Allow the Spirit to direct your prayer. Be open. Jesus speaks here and now. "I am..." In your hunger and thirst, who/what is the object?

  'I am the bread of life.
  He who comes to me will never be hungry;
  he who believes in me will never thirst.'

(Jn. 6:35)

POINTS

• Enter into the great mystery of the Eucharist. Jesus gives himself to us. He is our nourishment, our life. Allow the Father to reveal to you the mystery of his Son. He does this in quiet and peace.

  And as they were eating he took some bread, and when he had said the blessing he broke it and gave

it to them. 'Take it,' he said 'this is my body.' Then
he took a cup, and when he had returned thanks he
gave it to them, and all drank from it, and he said
to them, 'This is my blood, the blood of the
covenant, which is to be poured out for many. I tell
you solemnly, I shall not drink any more wine until
the day I drink the new wine in the kingdom of
God.'

(Mk. 14:22-25)

• Note Jesus' concern for the people. He is so sensitive and
generous. How conscious he is of the Father, that all comes from
him. The people and disciples are filled with amazement and
wonder. What love! What joy!

When Jesus received this news he withdrew by
boat to a lonely place where they could be by
themselves. But the people heard of this and,
leaving the towns, went after him on foot. So as he
stepped ashore he saw a large crowd; and he took
pity on them and healed their sick.

When evening came, the disciples went to him and
said, 'This is a lonely place, and the time has slipped
by; so send the people away, and they can go to the
villages to buy themselves some food.' Jesus replied,
'There is no need for them to go: give them
something to eat yourselves'. But they answered,
'All we have with us is five loaves and two fish'.
'Bring them here to me' he said. He gave orders
that the people were to sit down on the grass; then
he took the five loaves and the two fish, raised his
eyes to heaven and said the blessing. And breaking
the loaves he handed them to his disciples who
gave them to the crowds. They all ate as much as
they wanted, and they collected the scraps
remaining, twelve baskets full. Those who ate
numbered about five thousand men, to say nothing
of women and children.

(Mt. 14:13-21)

LITURGY
Join the universal Church in the preface of the Holy Eucharist:

At the last supper, as he sat at table with his

29

apostles, he offered himself to you as the spotless lamb, the acceptable gift that gives you perfect praise. Christ has given us this memorial of his passion to bring us its saving power until the end of time.

CONCLUSION

God's food contains every delight and satisfies every taste. Praise God for such a gift, the gift of himself.

How differently with your people! You gave them the food of angels, from heaven untiringly sending them bread already prepared, containing every delight, satisfying every taste.

(Wis. 16:20)

Second Hour —

Theme: Gratitude for all God's gifts.
Desire: To sense that all is given; there is nothing that we have not received.

INTRODUCTION

God is near. He communicates in word and sacrament. Prayer is listening and responding; a dwelling in silence before the face of the Father.

All creatures depend on you
to feed them throughout the year;
you provide the food they eat,
with generous hand you satisfy their hunger.

(Ps. 104:27-28)

POINTS

• Though there are many gifts, all come from God. What a variety! Why should there be envy? Thank God for your own giftedness and the gifts of others.

There is a variety of gifts but always the same Spirit; there are all sorts of service to be done, but always to the same Lord, working in all sorts of different ways in different people, it is the same God who is working in all of them. The particular way in which the Spirit is given to each person is for a good purpose. One may have the gift of

preaching with wisdom given him by the Spirit;
another may have the gift of preaching instruction
given him by the same Spirit; and another the gift
of faith given by the same Spirit; another again the
gift of healing, through this one Spirit; one, the
power of miracles; another, prophecy; another the
gift of recognising spirits; another the gift of
tongues and another the ability to interpret them.
All these are the work of one and the same Spirit,
who distributes different gifts to different people
just as he chooses.

(1 Cor. 12:4-11)

• The Lord indeed has done great things for us. Our spirits
can rejoice and glorify God. Humility is needed to realize that all
is given. Pride and avarice destroy the spirit of poverty.

And Mary said:
'My soul proclaims the greatness of the Lord
and my spirit exults in God my savior;
because he has looked upon his lowly handmaid.
Yes, from this day forward all generations
    will call me blessed,
for the Almighty has done great things for me.
Holy is his name,
and his mercy reaches from age to age
    for those who fear him.
He has shown the power of his arm,
he has routed the proud of heart.
He has pulled down princes from their thrones
    and exalted the lowly.
The hungry he has filled with good things,
    the rich sent empty away.
He has come to the help of Israel his servant,
    mindful of his mercy
—according to the promise he made
    to our ancestors—
of his mercy to Abraham
    and to his descendants for ever.'

(Lk. 1:46-55)

LITURGY
The Church clearly recognizes the source of all giftedness:

31

Father, you are holy indeed, and all creation rightly gives you praise. All life, all holiness comes from you through your Son, Jesus Christ our Lord, by the working of the Holy Spirit.

(Canon III)

CONCLUSION

We must keep our gifts in their right place. Recognize that all comes from the Father.

> Two things I beg of you,
>   do not grudge me them before I die:
> keep falsehood and lies far from me,
>   give me neither poverty nor riches,
> grant me only my share of bread to eat.

(Prov. 30:7-8)

Third Hour —

Theme: The Father's extravagant generosity.
Desire: To long for the Giver more than the gift(s).

INTRODUCTION

The Father knows our every need. He sends us his Spirit that we might say "Abba." Into the desert of our lives, he sends us water and bread. We will not die.

> They demanded food, he sent them quails,
> he satisfied them with the bread of heaven.

(Ps. 105:40)

POINTS

• Pray this passage slowly. Taste and relish these words. Is this really true? God invites us to a covenant relationship. What deep love dwells behind this invitation! Pray in silence and awe.

> Oh, come to the water all you who are thirsty;
> though you may have no money, come!
> Buy corn without money, and eat,
> and, at no cost, wine and milk.
> Why spend money on what is not bread,
> your wages on what fails to satisfy?
> Listen, listen to me, and you will have
>   good things to eat
> and rich food to enjoy.

Pay attention, come to me;
listen, and your soul will live.
With you I will make an everlasting covenant
out of the favours promised to David.
See, I have made of you a witness to the peoples,
a leader and a master of the nations.
See, you will summon a nation you never knew,
those unknown will come hurrying to you,
for the sake of Yahweh your God,
of the Holy One of Israel who will glorify you.

(Is. 55:1-5)

• The Father is true to his promise. Throughout history he provides for his people. He provides for you now in this hour of prayer. Ponder Zechariah's great prayer—from the heart.

His father Zechariah was filled with the Holy Spirit
and spoke this prophecy:
  'Blessed be the Lord, the God of Israel,
  for he has visited his people,
     he has come to their rescue
  and he has raised up for us a power for salvation
  in the House of his servant David,
  even as he proclaimed,
  by the mouth of his holy prophets
     from ancient time,
  that he would save us from our enemies
  and from the hands of all who hate us.
  Thus he shows mercy to our ancestors,
  thus he remembers his holy covenant,
  the oath he swore
  to our father Abraham
  that he would grant us, free from fear,
  to be delivered from the hands of our enemies,
  to serve him in holiness and virtue
  in his presence, all our days.'

(Lk. 1:67-75)

LITURGY
The creed calls to mind God's goodness:

We believe in one God, the Father, the Almighty,
maker of heaven and earth, of all that is seen and
unseen.

Like Paul, we must never stop thanking the Father for our many graces. Our constant song: "We praise and thank you, Father."

> I never stop thanking God for all the graces you have received through Jesus Christ.
>
> (1 Cor. 1:4)

Fourth Hour —
Theme: Our daily dependency on God.
Desire: To come to terms with our radical poverty.

INTRODUCTION

Join Moses in his dependency. *Each* day God will provide what is needed. Here is a call to trust in the Father now, at this moment of prayer. He will provide in his time and in his own way.

> Then Yahweh said to Moses, 'Now I will rain down bread for you from the heavens. Each day the people are to go out and gather the day's portion; I propose to test them in this way to see whether they will follow my law or not.
>
> (Ex. 16:4)

POINTS

• Our anxiety and worry is useless. God tends to our smallest needs. We must trust in his power and wisdom. Try to see what Jesus saw; allow him to reveal the Father to you. Pause in wonder and awe at such a caring Father.

> 'This is why I am telling you not to worry about your life and what you are going to eat, not about your body and how you are to clothe it. Surely life means more than food, and the body more than clothing! Look at the birds in the sky. They do not sow or reap or gather into barns; yet your heavenly Father feeds them. Are you not worth much more than they are? Can any of you, for all his worrying, add one single cubit to his span of life? And why worry about clothing? Think of the flowers growing in the fields; they never have to

34

work or spin; yet I assure you that not even
Solomon in all his regalia was robed like one of
these. Now if that is how God clothes the grass in
the field which is there today and thrown into the
furnace tomorrow, will he not much more look
after you, you men of little faith? So do not worry;
do not say, "What are we to eat? What are we to
drink? How are we to be clothed?" It is the pagans
who set their hearts on all these things. Your
heavenly Father knows you need them all. Set your
hearts on his kingdom first, and on his
righteousness, and all these other things will be
given you as well. So do not worry about
tomorrow: tomorrow will take care of itself. Each
day has enough trouble of its own.'

(Mt. 6:25-34)

• In deep quiet, pray this psalm with Jesus. Let him lead you;
let him explain its meaning. Lord, teach us to pray. Show us
how to center on the Father and not on ourselves.

Look after me, God, I take shelter in you.
To Yahweh you say, 'My Lord,
you are my fortune, nothing else but you',
yet to those pagan deities in the land,
'My princes, all my pleasure is in you'.
Their idols teem, after these they run:
shall I pour their blood-libations?—not I!
Take their names on my lips?—never!
Yahweh, my heritage, my cup,
you, and you only, hold my lot secure;
the measuring line marks out delightful places for me,
for me the heritage is superb indeed.
I bless Yahweh, who is my counsellor,
and in the night my inmost self instructs me;
I keep Yahweh before me always,
for with him at my right hand nothing can shake me.
So my heart exults, my very soul rejoices,
my body, too, will rest securely,
for you will not abandon my soul to Sheol,
nor allow the one you love to see the Pit;
you will reveal the path of life to me,

give me unbounded joy in your presence,
and at your right hand everlasting pleasures.

(Ps. 16:1-11)

LITURGY

Reflect prayerfully on the preface's introductory dialogue:

The Lord be with you.	And also with you.
Lift up your hearts.	We lift them up to the Lord.
Let us give thanks to the Lord our God.	It is right to give him thanks and praise.

CONCLUSION

We are totally gifted, thus totally poor. God gives all. Bring in the lyre and sing.

Sing to Yahweh in gratitude,
play the lyre for our God:
who covers the heavens with clouds,
to provide the earth with rain,
to produce fresh grass on the hillsides
and the plants that are needed by man,
who gives their food to the cattle
and to the young ravens when they cry.

(Ps. 147:7-9)

Day of Sorrow for Sin

"And forgive us our debts"

(Mt. 6 : 12)

First Hour —
> Theme: Sin: living outside the presence of God.
> Desire: To see the root of sin in my personal life.

INTRODUCTION

Prayer involves communication. It is a dialogue with God. He begins and we respond; he speaks his love and forgiveness. Ask for the grace to understand the mystery of sin.

> Have mercy on me, O God, in your goodness,
> in your great tenderness wipe away my faults;
> wash me clean of my guilt,
> purify me from my sin.

(Ps. 51:1-2)

POINTS

• Join John in the desert. What did he see? Why was he sent? Let these words soak in and really penetrate your heart. What happened then, happens now!

> In due course John the Baptist appeared; he preached in the wilderness of Judaea and this was his message: 'Repent, for the kingdom of heaven is

close at hand.' This was the man the prophet Isaiah
spoke of when he said:
   A voice cries in the wilderness:
   Prepare a way for the Lord,
   make his paths straight.
This man John wore a garment made of camel-hair
with a leather belt round his waist, and his food
was locusts and wild honey. Then Jerusalem and all
Judaea and the whole Jordan district made their
way to him, and as they were baptised by him in
the river Jordan they confessed their sins. But
when he saw a number of Pharisees and Sadducees
coming for baptism he said to them, 'Brood of
vipers, who warned you to fly from the retribution
that is coming? But if you are repentant, produce
the appropriate fruit, and do not presume to tell
yourselves, "We have Abraham for our father",
because, I tell you, God can raise children for
Abraham from these stones. Even now the axe is
laid to the roots of the trees, so that any tree
which fails to produce good fruits will be cut down
and thrown on the fire. I baptise you in water for
repentance, but the one who follows me is more
powerful than I am, and I am not fit to carry his
sandals; he will baptise you with the Holy Spirit
and fire. His winnowing-fan is in his hand; he will
clear his threshing-floor and gather his wheat into
the barn; but the chaff he will burn in a fire that
will never go out.'

                                        (Mt. 3:1-12)

• Job seems like a contemporary person. What is sin? How
does it show itself? What separates us from the Father? Sit with
Job. Take it all in. Then turn to the Father.

   Have I put all my trust in gold,
      from finest gold sought my security?
   Have I ever gloated over my great wealth,
      or the riches that my hands have won?
   Or has the sight of the sun in its glory,
      or the glow of the moon as it walked the sky,
   stolen my heart, so that my hand

blew them a secret kiss?
That too would be a criminal offence,
to have denied the supreme God.

(Job 31:24-28)

LITURGY
We acknowledge the source of forgiveness:

Lord, by your cross and resurrection,
you have set us free.
You are the savior of the world.

(Acclamation D)

CONCLUSION
Prayer has an imperative, a call to action. Isaiah speaks for
God: cease to sin, cease to live outside God's presence, do good.

Take your wrong-doing out of my sight.
Cease to do evil.
Learn to do good,
search for justice,
help the oppressed,
be just to the orphan,
plead for the widow.

(Is. 1:16-17)

Second Hour —
Theme: God's extravagant mercy.
Desire: To appreciate and not take God's forgiveness for
granted.

INTRODUCTION
God is a God of great tenderness. To him we come in awe and
wonder. He is present now to reveal our sin and his forgiveness.
Listen!

In your loving kindness, answer me, Yahweh,
in your great tenderness turn to me;
do not hide your face from your servant,
quick, I am in trouble, answer me;
come to my side, redeem me,
from so many enemies ransom me.

(Ps. 69:16-18)

• Go to the reception. Stand in the corner and watch what happens. Jesus is the God-man. Note the question; note the clarity and force of Jesus' response. Ponder.

> In his honour Levi held a great reception in his house, and with them at table was a large gathering of tax collectors and others. The Pharisees and their scribes complained to his disciples and said, 'Why do you eat and drink with tax collectors and sinners?' Jesus said to them in reply, 'It is not those who are well who need the doctor, but the sick. I have not come to call the virtuous, but sinners to repentance.'
>
> (Lk. 5:29-32)

• What a powerful and humble prayer. Pray it slowly, reflectively. Taste each word. Here is a prayer of true sorrow, deep honesty, and loving joy. No false fronts, no more deception.

> Happy the man whose fault is forgiven,
>   whose sin is blotted out;
> happy the man whom Yahweh
>   accuses of no guilt,
>   whose spirit is incapable of deceit!
> All the time I kept silent, my bones were wasting away
>   with groans, day in, day out;
> day and night your hand
>   lay heavy on me;
> my heart grew parched as stubble
>   in summer drought.
> At last I admitted to you I had sinned;
>   no longer concealing my guilt,
> I said 'I will go to Yahweh
>   and confess my fault'.
> And you, you have forgiven the wrong I did,
>   have pardoned my sin.
> That is why each of your servants prays to you
>   in time of trouble;
> even if the floods come rushing down,
>   they will never reach him.
> You are a hiding place for me,

40

you guard me when in trouble,
you surround me with songs of deliverance.

(Ps. 32:1-7)

The liturgy helps us to have the proper focus on sin:

Though we are sinners, we trust in your mercy and
love. Do not consider what we truly deserve, but
grant us your forgiveness.

(Canon I)

CONCLUSION

Etch this verse into your heart. This is God speaking to us.
We are called to live this in regard to others.

There will be no further need for neighbour to try
to teach neighbour,or brother to say to brother,
'Learn to know Yahweh!' No, they will all know
me, the least no less than the greatest—it is
Yahweh who speaks—since I will forgive their
iniquity and never call their sin to mind.

(Jer. 31:34)

Third Hour —

Theme: The Cross: the price of sin.
Desire: To measure all sin in terms of Calvary.

INTRODUCTION

Ask for the spirit of prayer. It is the Spirit who prays in us. Go
slowly. Allow the Lord to lead.

We have sinned quite as much as our fathers,
we have been wicked, we are guilty;
our ancestors in Egypt never grasped
the meaning of your marvels.

(Ps. 106:6-7)

POINTS

• Why is all this happening? Reflect on the collective and
personal sin of mankind. Taste the pain and agony of the Lord.
Here are the tragic consequences of freedom abused. The Son of
God dies for us.

When they reached the place called The Skull, they
crucified him there and the two criminals also, one

on the right, the other on the left. Jesus said,
'Father, forgive them; they do not know what they
are doing'. Then they cast lots to share out his
clothing.

(Lk. 22:33-34)

• Sit down with Paul and let him describe the heart of the Christian message. Then turn to the Father and respond from the heart.
Our sin means that we have turned our backs on the Father's love.
Yet he never turns from us; he is always coming — right now —
welcoming us and embracing us.

It is not easy to die even for a good man—though
of course for someone really worthy, a man might
be prepared to die—but what proves that God loves
us is that Christ died for us while we were still
sinners. Having died to make us righteous, is it
likely that he would now fail to save us from God's
anger? When we were reconciled to God by the
death of his Son, we were still enemies; now that
we have been reconciled, surely we may count on
being saved by the life of his Son? Not merely
because we have been reconciled but because we
are filled with joyful trust in God, through our
Lord Jesus Christ, through whom we have already
gained our reconciliation.

(Rom. 5:7-11)

LITURGY

Ponder the prayer of consecration:

Take this, all of you, and drink from it: this is the
cup of my blood, the blood of the new and
everlasting covenant. It will be shed for you and for
all men so that sins may be forgiven. Do this in
memory of me.

CONCLUSION

Fidelity to God and his ways is our vocation. We must not turn
from his love.

Take care your heart is not seduced, that you do not
go astray, serving other gods and worshipping them.

(Dt. 11:16)

Fourth Hour —

Theme: Reconciliation: means of forgiveness.

Desire: To be grateful for all moments of reconciliation, especially the gift of the sacrament.

INTRODUCTION

God's creative act is always in process. He is creating us now; forming, molding, prodding. Dwell in his presence. Listen! Surrender to his work.

God, create a clean heart in me,
put into me a new and constant spirit,
do not banish me from your presence,
do not deprive me of your holy spirit.

(Ps. 51:10-11)

POINTS

• No matter where we are—up a tree or underground—the Lord approaches and invites us to turn to him. Conversion is an ongoing process. The unredeemed areas of our hearts must be healed. Jesus comes now to heal and touch our lives.

He entered Jericho and was going through the town when a man whose name was Zacchaeus made his appearance; he was one of the senior tax collectors and a wealthy man. He was anxious to see what kind of man Jesus was, but he was too short and could not see him for the crowd; so he ran ahead and climbed a sycamore tree to catch a glimpse of Jesus who was to pass that way. When Jesus reached the spot he looked up and spoke to him: 'Zacchaeus, come down. Hurry, because I must stay at your house today.' And he hurried down and welcomed him joyfully. They all complained when they saw what was happening. 'He has gone to stay at a sinner's house' they said. But Zacchaeus stood his ground and said to the Lord, 'Look, sir, I am going to give half my property to the poor, and if I have cheated anybody I will pay him back four times the amount'. And Jesus said to him, 'Today salvation has come to this house, because this man too is a son of Abraham; for the Son of Man has come to seek out and save what was lost'.

(Lk. 19:1-10)

- Jesus is our means of forgiveness. We go to him to reach the Father. Paul reviews some facts for us. Listen and respond to God's workings.

> Do not forget, then, that there was a time when you were pagans physically, termed the Uncircumcised by those who speak of themselves as the Circumcision by reason of a physical operation, do not forget, I say, that you had no Christ and were excluded from membership of Israel, aliens with no part in the covenants,with their Promise; you were immersed in this world, without hope and without God. But now in Christ Jesus, you that used to be so far apart from us have been brought very close, by the blood of Christ. For he is the peace between us, and has made the two into one and broken down the barrier which used to keep them apart, actually destroying in his own person the hostility caused by the rules and decrees of the Law. This was to create one single New Man in himself out of the two of them and by restoring peace through the cross, to unite them both in a single Body and reconcile them with God. In his own person he killed the hostility. Later he came to bring the good news of peace, peace to you who were far away and peace to those who were near at hand. Through him, both of us have in the one Spirit our way to come to the Father.
>
> (Eph. 2:11-18)

LITURGY

Through the absolution formula in the rite of reconciliation, we have a rich theology of God's forgiveness and mercy:

> God, the Father of mercies, through the death and resurrection of his Son, has reconciled the world to himself and sent the Holy Spirit among us for the forgiveness of sin. Through the ministry of the Church, may God grant you pardon and peace; and I absolve you from your sins in the name of the Father, and of the Son, and of the Holy Spirit. Amen.

CONCLUSION

Our life is one of union with Christ.

...and this hope is not deceptive, because the love of God has been poured into our hearts by the Holy Spirit which has been given us. We were still helpless when at his appointed moment Christ died for sinful men. It is not easy to die even for a good man—though of course for someone really worthy, a man might be prepared to die—but what proves that God loves us is that Christ died for us while we were still sinners.

(Rom. 5:5-7)

Day of Gentleness and Compassion

"As we have forgiven those
who are in debt to us"

(Mt. 6:12)

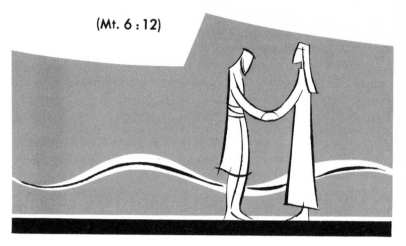

First Hour —

Theme: Wounded Healer.

Desire: To acknowledge and deal with our being hurt.

INTRODUCTION

Draw into the presence of God who is a God of love and forgiveness. He is here now. We must listen to his word. We must pause in his presence. God has forgiven us in Christ; we must forgive each other in the same way.

> Be friends with one another, and kind, forgiving
> each other as readily as God forgave you in Christ.
>
> (Eph. 4:32)

POINTS

• Notice the honesty of Peter. He sees a limit in terms of forgiveness. But Jesus' vision is different. He sees no limit to forgiveness. We cannot have this perspective without the gift of the Spirit, the Spirit of loving forgiveness and forgiving love.

> Then Peter went up to him and said, 'Lord, how
> often must I forgive my brother if he wrongs me?

46

As often as seven times?' Jesus answered, 'Not
seven, I tell you, but seventy-seven times.'

(Mt. 18:21-22)

• Paul's experience of being called to forgiveness. How are we
to respond when we are maltreated? What is our history of being
hurt? Our reactions?

When we are cursed, we answer with a blessing;
when we are hounded, we put up with it; we are
insulted and we answer politely. We are treated as
the offal of the world, still to this day, the scum of
the earth.

(1 Cor. 4:12-13)

LITURGY

Ponder this introduction to the Our Father in the liturgy:

Let us ask our Father to forgive our sins and to
bring us to forgive those who sin against us.

CONCLUSION

Here is a good summary statement of our call. Rest in the
Father's presence. Allow Jesus to pray to him through you.

Bear with one another; forgive each other as soon
as a quarrel begins. The Lord has forgiven you;
now you must do the same.

(Col. 3:13)

Second Hour —

Theme: The call to compassion and gentleness.
Desire: To imitate those who totally forgave.

INTRODUCTION

In prayer we commit our entire self to God. This is why
prayer and death are so similar and so difficult. Surrender now
to the Lord.

Pull me out of the net they have spread for me,
for you are my refuge;
into your hands I commit my spirit,
you have redeemed me, Yahweh.

(Ps. 31:4-5)

• Allow God to reveal the heart and mind of Stephen to you. How like Jesus he is! In deep silence listen, observe and then respond.

> But Stephen, filled with the Holy Spirit, gazed into heaven and saw the glory of God, and Jesus standing at God's right hand. 'I can see heaven thrown open' he said 'and the Son of Man standing at the right hand of God.' At this all the members of the council shouted out and stopped their ears with their hands; then they all rushed at him, sent him out of the city and stoned him. The witnesses put down their clothes at the feet of a young man called Saul. As they were stoning him, Stephen said in invocation, 'Lord Jesus, receive my spirit'. Then he knelt down and said aloud, 'Lord, do not hold this sin against them'; and with these words he fell asleep.
>
> (Acts 7:55-60)

• Jesus calls us to love those who hurt us, i.e., our enemies. Only compassion and gentleness in the Spirit will redeem. Love is the core.

> You have learnt how it was said: You must love your neighbour and hate your enemy. But I say this to you: love your enemies and pray for those who persecute you; in this way you will be sons of your Father in heaven, for he causes his sun to rise on bad men as well as good, and his rain to fall on honest and dishonest men alike. For if you love those who love you, what right have you to claim any credit? Even the tax collectors do as much, do they not? And if you save your greetings for your brothers, are you doing anything exceptional? Even the pagans do as much, do they not? You must therefore be perfect just as your heavenly Father is perfect.
>
> (Mt. 5:43-48)

LITURGY

God's eternal mercy and compassion are expressed in our public worship:

48

Even when he (man) disobeyed you and lost your friendship you did not abandon him to the power of death, but helped all men to seek and find you. Again and again you offered a covenant to man...

(Canon IV)

CONCLUSION

Here is the ideal. Jesus is our guide and model. Praise and thank the Father for our redemption.

Jesus said, 'Father, forgive them; they do not know what they are doing'. Then they cast lots to share out his clothing.

(Lk. 23:34)

Third Hour —

Theme: Anger and resentment.
Desire: To recognize these movements and to seek alternative responses.

INTRODUCTION

God is our center. In prayer we come to him in sincere honesty and purity. Purification of certain movements of our hearts must be dealt with. Job does ask the question; God helps us find the answer.

Have I taken pleasure in my enemies' misfortunes, or made merry when disaster overtook them...?

(Job 31:29)

POINTS

• Enter the scene. Here is the Son of God in contrast to the sons of men. How do they respond when hospitality is refused? The disciples completely misread what the Father is like. Jesus must correct their vision and their response.

Now as the time drew near for him to be taken up to heaven, he resolutely took the road for Jerusalem and sent messengers ahead of him. These set out, and they went into a Samaritan village to make preparations for him, but the people would not receive him because he was making for Jerusalem. Seeing this, the disciples James and John said, 'Lord, do you want us to call down fire from

49

heaven to burn them up?' But he turned and
rebuked them, and they went off to another village.

(Lk. 9:51-56)

• What a powerful experience this is! It still happens in our
lives today. What is Jesus' response? Anger? Resentment? We
are called to imitate our Lord.

They seized him then and led him away, and they
took him to the high priest's house. Peter followed
at a distance. They had lit a fire in the middle of
the courtyard and Peter sat down among them, and
as he was sitting there by the blaze a servant-girl
saw him, peered at him, and said, 'This person was
with him too'. But he denied it. 'Woman,' he said 'I
do not know him.' Shortly afterwards someone else
saw him and said, 'You are another of them'. But
Peter replied, 'I am not, my friend'. About an hour
later another man insisted, saying, 'This fellow was
certainly with him. Why, he is a Galilean.' 'My
friend,' said Peter 'I do not know what you are
talking about.' At that instant, while he was still
speaking, the cock crew, and the Lord turned and
looked straight at Peter, and Peter remembered
what the Lord had said to him, 'Before the cock
crows today, you will have disowned me three
times'. And he went outside and wept bitterly.

(Lk. 22:54-62)

LITURGY
We humbly come before the Lord in our sin:

Lamb of God, you take away the sin of the world,
have mercy on us.
Lamb of God, you take away the sin of the world,
have mercy on us.
Lamb of God, you take away the sin of the world,
grant us peace.

CONCLUSION
We must pray for the gift of forgiveness. Praise God for his
mercy and peace.

...because there will be judgement without mercy

for those who have not been merciful themselves;
but the merciful need have no fear of judgement.

(Jas. 2:13)

Fourth Hour —
>   Theme: The Spirit of Peace.
>   Desire: To live in God's peace, to be an instrument of it.

INTRODUCTION

Yahweh is so kind, forgiving, redeeming. Into his presence we
come in prayer. Listen and worship! Allow God to direct your
prayer. His presence is central.

>   Bless Yahweh, my soul,
>   and remember all his kindnesses:
>   in forgiving all your offences,
>   in curing all your diseases.

(Ps. 103:2-3)

POINTS

• Enter the room. Taste the fear. Then the surprise, the
peace, the being sent, the being gifted with the Spirit. God's
Spirit of peace is given in the face of sin.

>   In the evening of that same day, the first day of
>   the week, the doors were closed in the room where
>   the disciples were, for fear of the Jews. Jesus came
>   and stood among them. He said to them, 'Peace be
>   with you', and showed them his hands and his side.
>   The disciples were filled with joy when they saw
>   the Lord, and he said to them again, 'Peace be with
>   you.
>   'As the Father sent me,
>   so am I sending you.'
>   After saying this he breathed on them and said:
>   'Receive the Holy Spirit.
>   For those whose sins you forgive,
>   they are forgiven;
>   for those whose sins you retain,
>   they are retained.'

(Jn. 20:19-23)

- Peace comes with compassion and being non-judgmental, in pardoning and being pardoned. The call is to be like the Father. We are made to his image and likeness. By conforming to this we find happiness and peace.

'Be compassionate as your Father is compassionate. Do not judge, and you will not be judged yourselves; do not condemn, and you will not be condemned yourselves; grant pardon, and you will be pardoned. Give, and there will be gifts for you: a full measure, pressed down, shaken together, and running over, will be poured into your lap; because the amount you measure out is the amount you will be given back.'

(Lk. 6:36-38)

LITURGY

Turn to Jesus and experience his great gift:

Lord Jesus Christ, you said to your apostles: I leave you peace, my peace I give you. Look not on our sins, but on the faith of the Church, and grant us the peace and unity of your kingdom where you live for ever and ever. Amen.

CONCLUSION

Break into song. God's love is everlasting. What good news we have! This is our peace.

I sing your praises, God my King,
I bless your name for ever and ever,
blessing you day after day,
and praising your name for ever and ever.
Can anyone measure the magnificence
of Yahweh the great, and his inexpressible grandeur?

(Ps. 145:1-3)

Day of Discernment and Choice

"And do not put us to the test"

(Mt. 6:13)

First Hour —
    Theme: The reality of temptation.
    Desire: To perceive the spiritual dangers of life.

INTRODUCTION

Prayer is a call to listen. One temptation is to be too active; to equate prayer with talking. God leads and we are first to listen and only then to respond. God speaks now in scripture.

If only you would listen to him today,
'Do not harden your hearts as at Meribah,
as you did that day at Massah in the wilderness,
when your ancestors challenged me, tested me,
although they had seen what I could do.'

(Ps. 95:8-9)

POINTS

• The story of people drifting from the truth; drawn away from God's word. They take control and do their own thing. Then they will not own their action. What a vicious circle sin is. Allow God to reveal who you are in this account.

The man and his wife heard the sound of Yahweh

God walking in the garden in the cool of the day, and they hid from Yahweh God among the trees of the garden. But Yahweh God called to the man. 'Where are you?' he asked. 'I heard the sound of you in the garden;' he replied 'I was afraid because I was naked, so I hid.' 'Who told you that you were naked?' he asked 'Have you been eating of the tree I forbade you to eat?' The man replied, 'It was the woman you put with me; she gave me the fruit, and I ate it'. Then Yahweh God asked the woman, 'What is this you have done?' The woman replied, 'The serpent tempted me and I ate'.

(Gen. 3:8-13)

• Our Lord experienced spiritual dangers. What a battle! What attractions set before Jesus. We must be aware of the constant danger of idolatry. Allow the Father to show you your idols, what leads you astray.

Then Jesus was led by the Spirit out into the wilderness to be tempted by the devil. He fasted for forty days and forty nights, after which he was very hungry, and the tempter came and said to him, 'If you are the Son of God, tell these stones to turn into loaves'. But he replied, 'Scripture says:
Man does not live on bread alone
but on every word that comes
from the mouth of God'.

(Mt. 4:1-4)

LITURGY

The Church's prayer recognizes the reality of temptation:

We pray for our brothers and sisters who present themselves as catechumens. Keep far from them every evil spirit and all falsehood and sin, and they shall become temples of your Holy Spirit.

(Ritual)

CONCLUSION

God is to be trusted; our strength lies in him. No danger will be too great. He is near!

The trials that you have had to bear are no more than people normally have. You can trust God not

54

to let you be tried beyond your strength, and with
any trial he will give you a way out of it and the
strength to bear it.

(1 Cor. 10:13)

Second Hour —
> Theme: The gift of freedom.
> Desire: To own our choices and to assume responsibility
> for them.

INTRODUCTION

The Lord is with us and for us. Thus prayer is essentially a
joy: to be in loving company. God sets us free from all dangers.

> Hard-pressed, I invoked Yahweh,
> > he heard me and came to my relief.
> With Yahweh on my side, I fear nothing:
> > what can man do to me?
> With Yahweh on my side, best help of all,
> > I can triumph over my enemies.

(Ps. 118:5-7)

POINTS

• God gives us freedom to make the choices that Peter sets
before us. Not easy but in the Spirit we are empowered. How do I
use my freedom in these areas?

> Finally: you should all agree among yourselves and
> be sympathetic; love the brothers, have compassion
> and be self-effacing. Never pay back one wrong
> with another, or an angry word with another one;
> instead, pay back with a blessing. That is what you
> are called to do, so that you inherit a blessing
> yourself. Remember: Anyone who wants to have a
> happy life and to enjoy prosperity must banish
> malice from his tongue, deceitful conversation from
> his lips; he must never yield to evil but must
> practise good; he must seek peace and pursue it.
> Because the face of the Lord frowns on evil men,
> but the eyes of the Lord are turned toward the
> virtuous.

(1 Pet. 3:8-14)

• Jesus came to bring freedom. Enter the synagogue. Listen carefully. Taste the words. God's love and grace frees us, to be fully human.

He came to Nazara, where he had been brought up,
and went into the synagogue on the sabbath day
as he usually did. He stood up to read, and they
handed him the scroll of the prophet Isaiah.
Unrolling the scroll he found the place where it is
written:
The spirit of the Lord has been given to me,
for he has anointed me.
He has sent me to bring the good news to the poor,
to proclaim liberty to captives
and to the blind new sight,
to set the downtrodden free,
to proclaim the Lord's year of favour.
He then rolled up the scroll, gave it back to the
assistant and sat down. And all eyes in the
synagogue were fixed on him. Then he began to
speak to them, 'This text is being fulfilled today
even as you listen'. And he won the approval of all,
and they were astonished by the gracious words
that came from his lips.

(Lk. 4:16-22)

LITURGY

In the rite of confirmation, the Spirit is given to empower us:

Jesus Christ the Son of God promised that the
Spirit of truth would be with his Church forever:
may he bless you and give you courage in
professing the true faith.

CONCLUSION

Praise God for sending Jesus who frees us from all slaveries.

It was not for any fault on the part of creation that
it was made unable to attain its purpose, it was
made so by God; but creation still retains the hope
of being freed, like us, from its slavery to
decadence, to enjoy the same freedom and glory as
the children of God.

(Rom. 8:20-21)

Third Hour —
Theme: The call to discernment.
Desire: To foster a discerning heart like that of Jesus.

INTRODUCTION

In prayer we enter a covenant like Abraham. Discernment allows us to hear the voice of the Father. God is here. He speaks to us his message of love. Listen!

The Lord therefore promised him an oath
to bless the nations through his descendants,
to multiply him like the dust on the ground.

(Sir. 44:22)

POINTS

- What a powerful story! Abraham is tested. He discerns and will do whatever the Lord asks. What is our Isaac? How well do we sort out the things of God? Listen as God reveals Abraham's discerning heart.

Abraham took the wood for the burnt offering, loaded it on Isaac and carried in his own hands the fire and the knife. Then the two of them set out together. Isaac spoke to his father Abraham, 'Father' he said. 'Yes, my son' he replied. 'Look,' he said 'here are the fire and the wood, but where is the lamb for the burnt offering?' Abraham answered, 'My son, God himself will provide the lamb for the burnt offering'. Then the two of them went on together.

When they arrived at the place God had pointed out to him, Abraham built an altar there, and arranged the wood. Then he bound his son Isaac and put him on the altar on top of the wood. Abraham stretched out his hand and seized the knife to kill his son.

But the angel of Yahweh called to him from heaven. 'Abraham, Abraham' he said. 'I am here' he replied. 'Do not raise your hand against the boy' the angel said. 'Do not harm him, for now I know you fear God. You have not refused me your son, your only son.' Then looking up, Abraham saw a ram caught by its horns in a bush. Abraham took the ram and offered it as a burnt-offering in place

of his son. Abraham called this place 'Yahweh
provides', and hence the saying today: On the
mountain Yahweh provides.

(Gen. 22:6-14)

• Peter lacks discernment and must be corrected. Jesus
discerns that suffering is part of his Father's plan and he
embraces it. Peter wants a "rose garden Christianity." How
God's ways differ from man's! Ask for the gift of discernment.

From that time Jesus began to make it clear to his
disciples that he was destined to go to Jerusalem
and suffer grievously at the hands of the elders and
chief priests and scribes, to be put to death and to
be raised up on the third day. Then, taking him
aside, Peter started to remonstrate with him.
'Heaven preserve you, Lord;' he said 'this must not
happen to you'. But he turned and said to Peter,
'Get behind me, Satan! You are an obstacle in my
path, because the way you think is not God's way
but man's.

(Mt. 16:21-23)

LITURGY

The sequence of Pentecost recognizes the source of all our
gifts:

Give your seven holy gifts to your faithful, for
their trust is in you. Give them reward for their
virtuous acts; give them a death that ensures
salvation; give them unending bliss.

CONCLUSION

Testing is part of God's way. We must discern. Praise God for
making us grow through struggles.

It is not every spirit, my dear people,
    that you can trust;
test them, to see if they come from God;
there are many false prophets, now, in the world.
You can tell the spirits that come from God by this:
every spirit which acknowledges that Jesus the Christ
has come in the flesh is from God.

(1 Jn. 4:1-2)

58

Fourth Hour —
    Theme: Being led by the Spirit.
    Desire: To be open to the Spirit of the Father and the Son.

INTRODUCTION
  Jesus speaks and we are called to believe. Lord, strengthen our faith. He sends the Spirit of truth. He will lead us. Being led is the core of our life.

> But when the Spirit of truth comes
> he will lead you to the complete truth,
> since he will not be speaking as from himself
> but will say only what he has learnt;
> and he will tell you of the things to come.
>
>   (Jn. 16:13)

POINTS
  • Job's encounter with the Lord. He seeks the right relationship with God. Is this my prayer? How arrogant am I? Does the Lord lead or not?

> This was the answer Job gave to Yahweh:
>   I know that you are all-powerful:
>   what you conceive, you can perform.
>   I am the man who obscured your designs
>   with my empty-headed words.
>   I have been holding forth on matters I cannot
>   understand,
>   on marvels beyond me and my knowledge.
>   (Listen, I have more to say,
>   now it is my turn to ask questions and yours is
>   to inform me.)
>   I knew you then only by hearsay;
>   but now, having seen you with my own eyes,
>   I retract all I have said,
>   and in dust and ashes I repent.
>
>   (Job 42:1-6)

  • Note the obedience of Jesus. He is led by the Father. The emptying, the dying and the rising are fully accepted. We are to follow. Ponder, listen, praise God.

> His state was divine,
> yet he did not cling
> to his equality with God
> but emptied himself

59

to assume the condition of a slave,
and became as men are;
and being as all men are,
he was humbler yet,
even to accepting death,
death on a cross.
But God raised him high
and gave him the name
which is above all other names
so that all beings
in the heavens, on earth and in the underworld,
should bend the knee at the name of Jesus
and that every tongue should acclaim
Jesus Christ as Lord,
to the glory of God the Father.

(Phil. 2:6-11)

LITURGY

The preface of the Holy Spirit draws our attention to the role of the Spirit in our lives:

You gave us your Holy Spirit to help us always by his power, so that with loving trust we may turn to you in all our troubles, and give you thanks in all our joys, through Jesus...

CONCLUSION

Praise God for the way in which he trains and guides us. Revere and honor him. What a loving Father we have!

'Learn from this that Yahweh your God was training you as a man trains his child, and keep the commandments of Yahweh your God, and so follow his ways and reverence him.'

(Dt. 8:5-6)

Day of Rejoicing in Being Saved

"But save us from the evil one"

(Mt. 6:13)

The true Lamb who took away   ✕   the sins of the world

First Hour —
> Theme: God's saving love.
> Desire: To sense God's tangible, saving presence.

INTRODUCTION

In prayer we are led by God's Spirit. In listening and responding is our salvation. The Father reveals his path of righteousness in Jesus. "Listen and know that I am God."

> Yahweh, lead me in the path of your righteousness,
>> for there are men lying in wait for me;
> make your way plain before me.
>
> (Ps. 5:8)

POINTS

• People are on the road. Who will save them? Who will deliver and redeem these poor suffering human beings? Jesus is on the road. They meet. Salvation! Who returns to give thanks for the goodness of God?

> Now on the way to Jerusalem he travelled along the border between Samaria and Galilee. As he entered one of the villages, ten lepers came to meet him. They stood some way off and called to him,

'Jesus! Master! Take pity on us.' When he saw them he said, 'Go and show yourselves to the priests'. Now as they were going away they were cleansed. Finding himself cured, one of them turned back praising God at the top of his voice and threw himself at the feet of Jesus and thanked him. The man was a Samaritan. This made Jesus,say, 'Were not all ten made clean? The other nine, where are they? It seems that no one has come back to give praise to God, except this foreigner. And he said to the man, 'Stand up and go on your way. Your faith has saved you.'

(Lk. 17:11-19)

• A man is on the road. Someone searching for a deeper life. Jesus comes along and will save. Note the urgency of the moment. Note the sad, sad response. Life is so close.

He was setting out on a journey when a man ran up, knelt before him and put this question to him, 'Good master, what must I do to inherit eternal life?' Jesus said to him, 'Why do you call me good? No one is good but God alone. You know the commandments: You must not kill; You must not commit adultery; You must not steal; You must not bring false witness; You must not defraud; Honour your father and mother.' And he said to him, 'Master, I have kept all these from my earliest days'. Jesus looked steadily at him and loved him, and he said, 'There is one thing you lack. Go and sell everything you own and give the money to the poor, and you will have treasure in heaven; then come, follow me.' But his face fell at these words and he went away sad, for he was a man of great wealth.

(Mk. 10:17-22)

LITURGY

God's saving love is evidenced in this Easter preface:

He is the true Lamb
  who took away the sins of the world.
By dying he destroyed our death;
By rising he restored our life.

CONCLUSION

God holds us in such high esteem. Praise and thank the Father for his saving love.

> I look up at your heavens, made by your fingers,
> at the moon and stars you set in place—
> ah, what is man that you should
>   spare a thought for him,
> the son of man that you should care for him?
>
> (Ps. 8:3-4)

Second Hour —
>   Theme: The mystery of evil.
>   Desire: To deepen our understanding concerning the forms
>   of evil.

INTRODUCTION

Prayer is coming before the face of God. He bends down and listens. He reveals. He is quick to answer our every prayer. Come in faith and worship.

> Yahweh, hear my prayer,
> let my cry for help reach you;
> do not hide your face from me
> when I am in trouble;
> bend down to listen to me,
> when I call, be quick to answer me!
>
> (Ps. 102:1-2)

POINTS

• Jesus saw the evils of the future: mockery, physical beatings, being condemned. Sin is evil. Once we are outside God's presence anything can happen. How much darkness and evil exist in the world!

> Jesus was going up to Jerusalem, and on the way he took the Twelve to one side and said to them, 'Now we are going up to Jerusalem, and the Son of Man is about to be handed over to the chief priests and scribes. They will condemn him to death and will hand him over to the pagans to be mocked and scourged and crucified; and on the third day he will rise again.'
>
> (Mt. 20:17-19)

• Our healing comes from the woundedness of Christ. Ask the Father to reveal to you the mystery of Jesus' passion. What would our response have been to so much hatred?

This, in fact, is what you were called to do, because Christ suffered for you and left an example for you to follow the way he took. He had not done anything wrong, and there had been no perjury in his mouth. He was insulted and did not retaliate with insults; when he was tortured he made no threats but he put his trust in the righteous judge. He was bearing our faults in his own body on the cross, so that we might die to our faults and live for holiness; through his wounds you have been healed. You had gone astray like sheep but now you have come back to the shepherd and guardian of your souls.

(1 Pet. 2:21-24)

LITURGY
In Eucharist, we pray for deliverance:

Deliver us, Lord, from every evil, and grant us peace in our day.

CONCLUSION
Lord, let us live in your law and not follow evil paths.

Happy the man
who never follows the advice of the wicked
or loiters on the way that sinners take,
or sits about with scoffers,
but finds his pleasure in the Law of Yahweh,
and murmurs his law day and night.

(Ps. 1:1-2)

Third Hour —
Theme: Mission: called to save others.
Desire: To generously serve in continuing the work of Christ.

INTRODUCTION
God calls out in our daily life. Jeremiah heard and responded. In this hour of prayer the Father calls us. We too are to be

willing to serve and continue the work of delivering others from evil.

> The word of Yahweh was addressed to me, saying,
> 'Before I formed you in the womb I knew you;
> before you came to birth I consecrated you;
> I have appointed you as prophet to the nations.'
> I said, 'Ah, Lord Yahweh; look, I do not know
>   how to speak: I am a child!'
> But Yahweh replied,
> 'Do not say, "I am a child".
> Go now to those to whom I send you
> and say whatever I command you.'

(Jer. 1:4-7)

POINTS

- Enter into this mystery. These words are addressed to you. The good news confronts evil and delivers the powerless. The key: "I am with you always." Herein lies our strength and hope.

> Meanwhile the eleven disciples set out for Galilee, to the mountain where Jesus had arranged to meet them. When they saw him they fell down before him, though some hesitated. Jesus came up and spoke to them. He said, 'All authority in heaven and on earth has been given to me. Go, therefore, make disciples of all the nations; baptise them in the name of the Father and of Son and of the Holy Spirit, and teach them to observe all the commands I gave you. And know that I am with you always; yes, to the end of time.'

(Mt. 28:16-20)

- To be a loving and caring person is to do the work of Jesus. God is love. He who loves makes God present. Love delivers and heals and restores. We are caught up in this process. What a responsibility! What a privilege!

> But the man was anxious to justify himself and said to Jesus, 'And who is my neighbour?' Jesus replied, 'A man was once on his way down from Jerusalem to Jericho and fell into the hands of brigands; they took all he had, beat him and then made off, leaving him half dead. Now a priest happened to be travelling down the same road, but when he saw

the man, he passed by on the other side. In the same way a Levite who came to the place saw him, and passed by on the other side. But a Samaritan traveller who came upon him was moved with compassion when he saw him. He went up and bandaged his wounds, pouring oil and wine on them. He then lifted him on to his own mount, carried him to the inn and looked after him. Next day, he took out two denarii and handed them to the innkeeper. "Look after him," he said "and on my way back I will make good any extra expense you have." Which of these three, do you think, proved himself a neighbour to the man who fell into the brigands' hands?' 'The one who took pity on him' he replied. Jesus said to him, 'Go, and do the same yourself'.

(Lk. 10:29-37)

LITURGY

In worship we are called to continue and complete the work of Jesus:

And that we might live no longer for ourselves but for him, he sent the Holy Spirit from you, Father, as his first gift to those who believe, to complete his work on earth, and bring us the fulness of grace.

(Canon IV)

CONCLUSION

Praise the Father for gracing Isaiah to respond so well. Pray that we might follow the prophets and the Prophet.

Then I heard the voice of the Lord saying:
'Whom shall I send? Who will be our messenger?'
I answered, 'Here I am, send me'. He said:
'Go and say to this people,
"Hear and hear again, but do not understand;
see and see again, but do not perceive".'

(Is. 6:8-9)

Fourth Hour —
Theme: The kingdom realized — Evil is overcome —
the Banquet.
Desire: To have a vision of what our goal of redemption is.

INTRODUCTION
Note Paul's deep desire. Our prayer at bottom is to know
Jesus. This leads us to the Father. In prayer, the Father reveals
his Son; the Son shows us the Father.

All I want is to know Christ and the power of his
resurrection and to share his sufferings by
reproducing the pattern of his death. This is the
way I can hope to take my place in the resurrection
of the dead.

(Phil. 3:10-11)

POINTS
• Be at table with the Lord. The kingdom happens now. We
are called to recognize the Lord, to rejoice in his presence. Sit at
table and experience the Lord.

When they drew near to the village to which they
were going, he made as if to go on; but they
pressed him to stay with them. 'It is nearly evening'
they said 'and the day is almost over.' So he went
in to stay with them. Now while he was with them
at table, he took the bread and said the blessing;
then he broke it and handed it to them. And their
eyes were opened and they recognized him; but he
had vanished from their sight. Then they said to
each other, 'Did not our hearts burn within us as
he talked to us on the road and explained the
scriptures to us?'

(Lk. 24:28-32)

• Join this group, so human and warm, at the morning
breakfast. The invitation to sit and eat — Eucharist. Note the
intimacy and love.

As soon as they came ashore they saw that there
was some bread there, and a charcoal fire with fish
cooking on it. Jesus said, 'Bring some of the fish
you have just caught'. Simon Peter went aboard
and dragged the net to the shore, full of big fish,

one hundred and fifty-three of them; and in spite
of there being so many the net was not broken.
Jesus said to them, 'Come and have breakfast'.
None of the disciples was bold enough to ask, 'Who
are you?; they knew quite well it was the Lord.
Jesus then stepped forward, took the bread and
gave it to them, and the same with the fish. This
was the third time that Jesus showed himself to the
disciples after rising from the dead.

(Jn. 21:9-14)

LITURGY

Together we acclaim the mystery of our faith:

When we eat this bread and drink this cup,
we proclaim your death, Lord Jesus,
until you come in glory.

(Acclamation C)

CONCLUSION

We are born to sing a song of thanksgiving and praise. All
this is based on God's marvelous deeds. Lord, we praise and
thank you always. You have redeemed us and brought us home.

I thank you, Yahweh, with all my heart;
I recite your marvels one by one,
I rejoice and exult in you,
I sing praise to your name, Most High.

(Ps. 9-10:1-2)

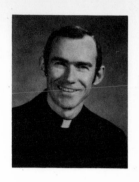

The AUTHOR

Father Robert F. Morneau was ordained to the priesthood in 1966 for the Diocese of Green Bay, Wisconsin. He has served as Diocesan Vicar for Religious, instructor of philosophy at Silver Lake College in Manitowoc, and associate pastor of Holy Redeemer Parish in Two Rivers. Fr. Morneau has also directed retreats and taught at the summertime Theological Institute of St. Norbert's College, De Pere. His previous publications include articles in *Sisters Today, Review for Religious, Spiritual Life,* and *Contemplative Review.*

In December, 1978, shortly after the publication of this book, Fr. Morneau was named auxiliary bishop of the Green Bay Diocese. He was consecrated on February 22, 1979.

Art work is by Brother Placid Stuckenschneider, O.S.B.